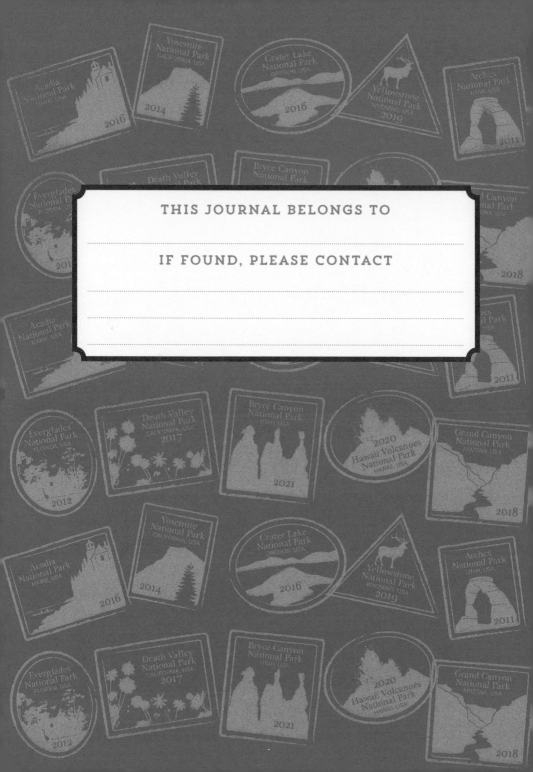

THIS JOURNAL BELONGS TO

....

IF FOUND, PLEASE CONTACT

....

....

....

USA
NATIONAL
PARKS
JOURNAL
=and=
PASSPORT STAMP BOOK

Peter Pauper Press, Inc.
WHITE PLAINS, NEW YORK

PETER PAUPER PRESS
Fine Books and Gifts Since 1928

Our Company

In 1928, at the age of twenty-two, Peter Beilenson began printing books on a small press in the basement of his parents' home in Larchmont, New York. Peter—and later, his wife, Edna—sought to create fine books that sold at "prices even a pauper could afford."

Today, still family owned and operated, Peter Pauper Press continues to honor our founders' legacy—and our customers' expectations—of beauty, quality, and value.

Designed by David Cole Wheeler
Images used under license from Shutterstock.com

Copyright © 2021
Peter Pauper Press, Inc.
202 Mamaroneck Avenue
White Plains, NY 10601
All rights reserved
ISBN 978-1-4413-3734-4
Printed in China
7 6 5 4 3 2

TABLE OF CONTENTS

INTRODUCTION

The United States hosts over 400 beautiful parks, historical sites, and memorials across its vast and varied expanse. Each national park contains treasures of nature and culture, just waiting to be explored. While this journal doesn't contain every national park in the country, it contains a selection of the most well-known and well-traveled sites of each state, the District of Columbia, and Puerto Rico, meant to entice you to explore the vast beauty of our nation.

Treat each spread as an adventure log. When you arrive at each park, flip to its corresponding page and jot down your memories and experiences. Each spread also contains a space to collect each park's passport stamp, with extra pages in the back for further travels. Once complete, this book will become a keepsake chronicling your adventures through all fifty states and beyond.

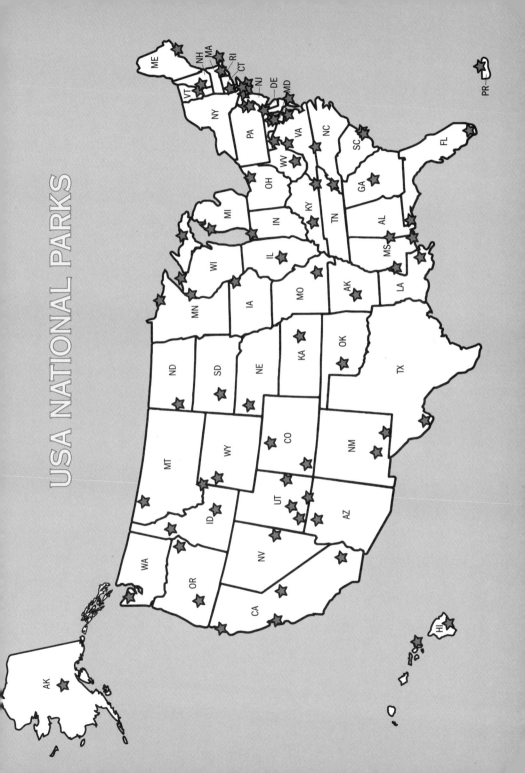

ACADIA NATIONAL PARK, ME

Date visited: .... Weather: ☀ 🌦 ☁ ⛅ 🌧 ⛈ ☁ 🌨 🌨

Traveling companions: ....

Where we stayed: ....

What we did: ....

....

....

Sights seen: ....

....

....

Wildlife seen: ....

....

....

Favorite moments: ....

....

....

....

....

....

....

....

....

....

PASSPORT STAMP(S)

Favorite attractions:

Visit again?

Things to remember for next time:

Park rating: ☆ ☆ ☆ ☆ ☆

NOTES AND PHOTOS

APOSTLE ISLANDS
NATIONAL LAKESHORE, WI

Date visited: .... Weather: ☀ ⛅ ☁ ⛅ 🌧 ⛈ ☁ 🌨 🌨

Traveling companions: ....

Where we stayed: ....

What we did: ....

....

....

....

Sights seen: ....

....

....

Wildlife seen: ....

....

....

Favorite moments: ....

....

....

....

....

....

....

....

....

PASSPORT STAMP(S)

Favorite attractions:

Visit again?

Things to remember for next time:

Park rating: ☆ ☆ ☆ ☆ ☆

NOTES AND PHOTOS

APPALACHIAN NATIONAL SCENIC TRAIL

Date visited: .... Weather: ☀ ⛅ ☁ ⛅ 🌧 ⛈ ☁ 🌨 🌨

Traveling companions: ....

Where we stayed: ....

What we did: ....

....

....

....

Sights seen: ....

....

....

Wildlife seen: ....

....

....

Favorite moments: ....

....

....

....

....

....

....

....

....

....

....

PASSPORT STAMP(S)

Favorite attractions:

Visit again?

Things to remember for next time:

Park rating: ☆ ☆ ☆ ☆ ☆

NOTES AND PHOTOS

ARCHES NATIONAL PARK, UT

Date visited: .... Weather: ☀ ⛅ ☁ ⛅ 🌧 ⛈ ☁ 🌨 🌨

Traveling companions: ....

Where we stayed: ....

What we did: ....

....

....

....

Sights seen: ....

....

....

....

Wildlife seen: ....

....

....

....

Favorite moments: ....

....

....

....

....

....

....

....

....

....

....

PASSPORT STAMP(S)

Favorite attractions:

Visit again?

Things to remember for next time:

Park rating: ☆ ☆ ☆ ☆ ☆

NOTES AND PHOTOS

ASSATEAGUE ISLAND
NATIONAL SEASHORE, MD/VA

Date visited: .... Weather:

Traveling companions: ....

Where we stayed: ....

What we did: ....

....

....

Sights seen: ....

....

....

Wildlife seen: ....

....

....

Favorite moments: ....

....

....

....

....

....

....

....

....

....

PASSPORT STAMP(S)

Favorite attractions:

Visit again?

Things to remember for next time:

Park rating: ☆ ☆ ☆ ☆ ☆

NOTES AND PHOTOS

BADLANDS NATIONAL PARK, SD

Date visited: .... Weather: ☀ ⛅ ☁ ⛅ 🌧 ⛈ ☁ ❄ 🌨

Traveling companions: ....

Where we stayed: ....

What we did: ....

....

....

....

Sights seen: ....

....

....

Wildlife seen: ....

....

....

Favorite moments: ....

....

....

....

....

....

....

....

....

....

PASSPORT STAMP(S)

Favorite attractions:

Visit again?

Things to remember for next time:

Park rating: ☆ ☆ ☆ ☆ ☆

NOTES AND PHOTOS

BIG BEND NATIONAL PARK, TX

Date visited: .... Weather: ☀ ⛅ ☁ ⛅ 🌧 ⛈ ☁ 🌨 🌨

Traveling companions: ....

Where we stayed: ....

What we did: ....

....

....

....

Sights seen: ....

....

....

Wildlife seen: ....

....

....

Favorite moments: ....

....

....

....

....

....

....

....

....

....

PASSPORT STAMP(S)

Favorite attractions:

Visit again?

Things to remember for next time:

Park rating: ☆ ☆ ☆ ☆ ☆

NOTES AND PHOTOS

BLUE RIDGE PARKWAY, NC/VA

Date visited: .... Weather: ☀ ⛅ ☁ ⛅ 🌧 ⛈ ☁ 🌨 🌨

Traveling companions: ....

Where we stayed: ....

What we did: ....

....

....

Sights seen: ....

....

....

Wildlife seen: ....

....

....

Favorite moments: ....

....

....

....

....

....

....

....

....

PASSPORT STAMP(S)

Favorite attractions:

Visit again?

Things to remember for next time:

Park rating:

NOTES AND PHOTOS

BRYCE CANYON NATIONAL PARK, UT

Date visited: ....

Weather: ☀ ⛅ ☁ ⛅ 🌧 ⛈ ☁ 🌨 🌨

Traveling companions: ....

Where we stayed: ....

What we did: ....

....

....

Sights seen: ....

....

....

Wildlife seen: ....

....

....

Favorite moments: ....

....

....

....

....

....

....

....

....

....

PASSPORT STAMP(S)

Favorite attractions:

Visit again?

Things to remember for next time:

Park rating: ☆ ☆ ☆ ☆ ☆

NOTES AND PHOTOS

CAPE COD NATIONAL SEASHORE, MA

Date visited: .... Weather: ☀ ⛅ ☁ ⛅ 🌧 ⛈ ☁ 🌨 🌨

Traveling companions: ....

Where we stayed: ....

What we did: ....

....

....

....

Sights seen: ....

....

....

....

Wildlife seen: ....

....

....

....

Favorite moments: ....

....

....

....

....

....

....

....

....

....

....

PASSPORT STAMP(S)

Favorite attractions:

Visit again?

Things to remember for next time:

Park rating: ☆ ☆ ☆ ☆ ☆

NOTES AND PHOTOS

CARLSBAD CAVERNS NATIONAL PARK, NM

Date visited: .... Weather: ☀ ⛅ ☁ ⛅ ☁ ⛈ ☁ 🌨 🌨

Traveling companions: ....

Where we stayed: ....

What we did: ....

....

....

....

Sights seen: ....

....

....

Wildlife seen: ....

....

....

Favorite moments: ....

....

....

....

....

....

....

....

....

....

PASSPORT STAMP(S)

Favorite attractions:

Visit again?

Things to remember for next time:

Park rating:

NOTES AND PHOTOS

CHESAPEAKE & OHIO CANAL
NATIONAL HISTORICAL PARK, DC/MD/WV

Date visited: .... Weather: ☀ ⛅ ☁ ⛅ 🌧 ⛈ ☁ 🌨 🌨

Traveling companions: ....

Where we stayed: ....

What we did: ....

....

....

Sights seen: ....

....

....

Wildlife seen: ....

....

....

Favorite moments: ....

....

....

....

....

....

....

....

....

....

PASSPORT STAMP(S)

Favorite attractions:

Visit again?

Things to remember for next time:

Park rating: ☆ ☆ ☆ ☆ ☆

NOTES AND PHOTOS

CRATER LAKE NATIONAL PARK, OR

Date visited: _____ Weather: ☀ ⛅ ☁ ⛅ 🌧 ⛈ ☁ 🌨 🌧

Traveling companions: _____

Where we stayed: _____

What we did: _____

_____

_____

_____

Sights seen: _____

_____

_____

Wildlife seen: _____

_____

_____

Favorite moments: _____

_____

_____

_____

_____

_____

_____

_____

_____

_____

_____

PASSPORT STAMP(S)

Favorite attractions:

Visit again?

Things to remember for next time:

Park rating: ☆ ☆ ☆ ☆ ☆

NOTES AND PHOTOS

CRATERS OF THE MOON
NATIONAL MONUMENT, ID

Date visited: .... Weather: ☀ ⛅ ☁ ⛅ 🌧 ⛈ ☁ 🌨 🌨

Traveling companions: ....

Where we stayed: ....

What we did: ....

....

....

....

Sights seen: ....

....

....

Wildlife seen: ....

....

....

Favorite moments: ....

....

....

....

....

....

....

....

....

PASSPORT STAMP(S)

Favorite attractions:

Visit again?

Things to remember for next time:

Park rating: ☆ ☆ ☆ ☆ ☆

NOTES AND PHOTOS

CUMBERLAND GAP
NATIONAL HISTORICAL PARK, KY/TN/VA

Date visited: .... Weather: ☀ 🌦 ☁ ⛅ 🌧 ⛈ ☁ 🌨 🌨

Traveling companions: ....

Where we stayed: ....

What we did: ....

....

....

....

....

Sights seen: ....

....

....

....

Wildlife seen: ....

....

....

....

....

Favorite moments: ....

....

....

....

....

....

....

....

....

....

....

PASSPORT STAMP(S)

Favorite attractions:

Visit again?

Things to remember for next time:

Park rating: ☆ ☆ ☆ ☆ ☆

NOTES AND PHOTOS

CUYAHOGA VALLEY NATIONAL PARK, OH

Date visited: .... Weather: ☀ ⛅ ☁ ⛅ 🌧 ⛈ ☁ 🌨 🌨

Traveling companions: ....

Where we stayed: ....

What we did: ....

....

....

....

Sights seen: ....

....

....

Wildlife seen: ....

....

....

Favorite moments: ....

....

....

....

....

....

....

....

....

....

PASSPORT STAMP(S)

Favorite attractions:

Visit again?

Things to remember for next time:

Park rating: ☆ ☆ ☆ ☆ ☆

NOTES AND PHOTOS

DELAWARE WATER GAP
NATIONAL RECREATION AREA, NJ/PA

Date visited: .... Weather:

Traveling companions: ....

Where we stayed: ....

What we did: ....

....

....

....

Sights seen: ....

....

....

....

Wildlife seen: ....

....

....

....

Favorite moments: ....

....

....

....

....

....

....

....

....

....

PASSPORT STAMP(S)

Favorite attractions:

Visit again?

Things to remember for next time:

Park rating: ☆ ☆ ☆ ☆ ☆

NOTES AND PHOTOS

DENALI NATIONAL PARK, AK

Date visited: .... Weather: ☀ ⛅ ☁ ⛅ 🌧 ⛈ ☁ 🌨 🌨

Traveling companions: ....

Where we stayed: ....

What we did: ....

....

....

....

Sights seen: ....

....

....

Wildlife seen: ....

....

....

Favorite moments: ....

....

....

....

....

....

....

....

....

PASSPORT STAMP(S)

Favorite attractions:

Visit again?

Things to remember for next time:

Park rating: ☆ ☆ ☆ ☆ ☆

NOTES AND PHOTOS

EFFIGY MOUNDS
NATIONAL MONUMENT, IA

Date visited: .... Weather: ☀ ⛈ ☁ ⛅ 🌧 ⛈ ☁ 🌨 🌨

Traveling companions: ....

Where we stayed: ....

What we did: ....

....

....

....

Sights seen: ....

....

....

Wildlife seen: ....

....

....

Favorite moments: ....

....

....

....

....

....

....

....

....

....

PASSPORT STAMP(S)

Favorite attractions:

Visit again?

Things to remember for next time:

Park rating: ☆ ☆ ☆ ☆ ☆

NOTES AND PHOTOS

ELLIS ISLAND/STATUE OF LIBERTY NATIONAL MONUMENT, NJ/NY

Date visited: .... Weather: ☀ ⛅ ☁ ⛅ ☁ ⛈ ☁ ☁ ☁

Traveling companions: ....

Where we stayed: ....

What we did: ....

....

....

Sights seen: ....

....

....

Wildlife seen: ....

....

....

Favorite moments: ....

....

....

....

....

....

....

....

....

....

PASSPORT STAMP(S)

Favorite attractions:

Visit again?

Things to remember for next time:

Park rating: ☆ ☆ ☆ ☆ ☆

NOTES AND PHOTOS

EVERGLADES NATIONAL PARK, FL

Date visited: .... Weather: ☀ ⛅ ☁ ⛅ 🌧 ⛈ ☁ 🌨 🌨

Traveling companions: ....

Where we stayed: ....

What we did: ....

....

....

Sights seen: ....

....

....

Wildlife seen: ....

....

....

Favorite moments: ....

....

....

....

....

....

....

....

....

....

....

PASSPORT STAMP(S)

Favorite attractions: ....

....

....

Visit again? ....

Things to remember for next time: ....

....

....

Park rating: ☆ ☆ ☆ ☆ ☆

NOTES AND PHOTOS

FIRST STATE
NATIONAL HISTORICAL PARK, DE/PA

Date visited: _____ Weather: ☀ ⛅ ☁ ⛅ 🌧 ⛈ ☁ 🌨 🌨

Traveling companions: _____

Where we stayed: _____

What we did: _____

_____

_____

_____

Sights seen: _____

_____

_____

Wildlife seen: _____

_____

_____

Favorite moments: _____

_____

_____

_____

_____

_____

_____

_____

_____

_____

PASSPORT STAMP(S)

Favorite attractions:

Visit again?

Things to remember for next time:

Park rating: ☆ ☆ ☆ ☆ ☆

NOTES AND PHOTOS

FORT SUMTER AND FORT MOULTRIE NATIONAL HISTORIC PARK, SC

Date visited: .... Weather: ☀ ⛅ ☁ ⛅ 🌧 ⛈ ☁ ❄ 🌨

Traveling companions: ....

Where we stayed: ....

What we did: ....

....

....

....

Sights seen: ....

....

....

....

Wildlife seen: ....

....

....

....

Favorite moments: ....

....

....

....

....

....

....

....

....

....

PASSPORT STAMP(S)

Favorite attractions:

Visit again?

Things to remember for next time:

Park rating: ☆ ☆ ☆ ☆ ☆

NOTES AND PHOTOS

GATEWAY
NATIONAL RECREATION AREA, NJ/NY

Date visited: _____ Weather: ☀ ⛅ ☁ ⛅ ☁ ⛈ ☁ ☁ ☁

Traveling companions: _____

Where we stayed: _____

What we did: _____

_____

_____

_____

Sights seen: _____

_____

_____

Wildlife seen: _____

_____

_____

Favorite moments: _____

_____

_____

_____

_____

_____

_____

_____

_____

_____

_____

PASSPORT STAMP(S)

Favorite attractions:

Visit again?

Things to remember for next time:

Park rating: ☆ ☆ ☆ ☆ ☆

NOTES AND PHOTOS

GLACIER NATIONAL PARK, MT

Date visited: .... Weather: ☀ ⛅ ☁ ⛅ 🌧 ⛈ ☁ 🌨 🌨

Traveling companions: ....

Where we stayed: ....

What we did: ....

....

....

Sights seen: ....

....

....

Wildlife seen: ....

....

....

Favorite moments: ....

....

....

....

....

....

....

....

PASSPORT STAMP(S)

Favorite attractions:

Visit again?

Things to remember for next time:

Park rating: ☆ ☆ ☆ ☆ ☆

NOTES AND PHOTOS

GLEN CANYON
NATIONAL RECREATION AREA, UT/AZ

Date visited: _____ Weather: ☀ ⛅ ☁ ⛅ 🌧 ⛈ ☁ 🌨 🌨

Traveling companions: _____

Where we stayed: _____

What we did: _____

_____

_____

_____

Sights seen: _____

_____

_____

Wildlife seen: _____

_____

_____

Favorite moments: _____

_____

_____

_____

_____

_____

_____

_____

_____

PASSPORT STAMP(S)

Favorite attractions:

Visit again?

Things to remember for next time:

Park rating: ☆ ☆ ☆ ☆ ☆

NOTES AND PHOTOS

GRAND CANYON NATIONAL PARK, AZ

Date visited: .... Weather: ☀ 🌦 ☁ ⛅ 🌧 ⛈ ☁ 🌨 🌨

Traveling companions: ....

Where we stayed: ....

What we did: ....

....

....

....

Sights seen: ....

....

....

....

Wildlife seen: ....

....

....

....

Favorite moments: ....

....

....

....

....

....

....

....

....

PASSPORT STAMP(S)

Favorite attractions:

Visit again?

Things to remember for next time:

Park rating: ☆ ☆ ☆ ☆ ☆

NOTES AND PHOTOS

GRAND TETON NATIONAL PARK, WY

Date visited: _____ Weather: ☀ 🌦 ☁ ⛅ 🌧 ⛈ 🌥 🌨 🌧

Traveling companions: _____

Where we stayed: _____

What we did: _____

_____

_____

_____

Sights seen: _____

_____

_____

Wildlife seen: _____

_____

_____

Favorite moments: _____

_____

_____

_____

_____

_____

_____

_____

_____

PASSPORT STAMP(S)

Favorite attractions:

Visit again?

Things to remember for next time:

Park rating: ☆ ☆ ☆ ☆ ☆

NOTES AND PHOTOS

GREAT BASIN NATIONAL PARK, NV

Date visited: ....

Weather:

Traveling companions: ....

Where we stayed: ....

What we did: ....

....

....

....

Sights seen: ....

....

....

Wildlife seen: ....

....

....

Favorite moments: ....

....

....

....

....

....

....

....

....

....

....

PASSPORT STAMP(S)

Favorite attractions:

Visit again?

Things to remember for next time:

Park rating: ☆ ☆ ☆ ☆ ☆

NOTES AND PHOTOS

GREAT SMOKY MOUNTAINS NATIONAL PARK, NC/TN

Date visited: .... Weather: ☀ ⛅ ☁ ⛅ ☁ ⛈ ☁ ☁ ☁

Traveling companions: ....

Where we stayed: ....

What we did: ....

....

....

....

Sights seen: ....

....

....

Wildlife seen: ....

....

....

Favorite moments: ....

....

....

....

....

....

....

....

....

....

PASSPORT STAMP(S)

Favorite attractions:

Visit again?

Things to remember for next time:

Park rating: ☆ ☆ ☆ ☆ ☆

NOTES AND PHOTOS

GULF ISLANDS
NATIONAL SEASHORE, FL/MS

Date visited: .... Weather: ☀ ⛅ ☁ ⛅ 🌧 ⛈ ☁ 🌨 🌨

Traveling companions: ....

Where we stayed: ....

What we did: ....

....

....

Sights seen: ....

....

....

Wildlife seen: ....

....

....

Favorite moments: ....

....

....

....

....

....

....

....

....

....

PASSPORT STAMP(S)

Favorite attractions:

Visit again?

Things to remember for next time:

Park rating: ☆ ☆ ☆ ☆ ☆

NOTES AND PHOTOS

HALEAKALĀ NATIONAL PARK, HI

Date visited: .... Weather: ☀ ⛈ ☁ ⛅ 🌧 ⛈ ☁ 🌨 🌨

Traveling companions: ....

Where we stayed: ....

What we did: ....

....

....

....

Sights seen: ....

....

....

Wildlife seen: ....

....

....

Favorite moments: ....

....

....

....

....

....

....

....

....

....

PASSPORT STAMP(S)

Favorite attractions:

Visit again?

Things to remember for next time:

Park rating: ☆ ☆ ☆ ☆ ☆

NOTES AND PHOTOS

HAWAI'I VOLCANOES NATIONAL PARK, HI

Date visited: .... Weather: ☀ ⛅ ☁ ⛅ 🌧 ⛈ ☁ 🌨 🌨

Traveling companions: ....

Where we stayed: ....

What we did: ....

....

....

....

Sights seen: ....

....

....

....

Wildlife seen: ....

....

....

....

Favorite moments: ....

....

....

....

....

....

....

....

....

....

....

PASSPORT STAMP(S)

Favorite attractions:

Visit again?

Things to remember for next time:

Park rating:

NOTES AND PHOTOS

HOT SPRINGS NATIONAL PARK, AR

Date visited: .... Weather:

Traveling companions: ....

Where we stayed: ....

What we did: ....

....

....

....

Sights seen: ....

....

....

Wildlife seen: ....

....

....

Favorite moments: ....

....

....

....

....

....

....

....

....

....

....

PASSPORT STAMP(S)

Favorite attractions:

Visit again?

Things to remember for next time:

Park rating: ☆ ☆ ☆ ☆ ☆

NOTES AND PHOTOS

INDEPENDENCE
NATIONAL HISTORICAL PARK, PA

Date visited: .... Weather: ☀ ⛅ ☁ ⛅ ☁ ⛈ ☁ 🌨 🌨

Traveling companions: ....

Where we stayed: ....

What we did: ....

....

....

....

Sights seen: ....

....

....

Wildlife seen: ....

....

....

Favorite moments: ....

....

....

....

....

....

....

....

....

....

PASSPORT STAMP(S)

Favorite attractions:

Visit again?

Things to remember for next time:

Park rating: ☆ ☆ ☆ ☆ ☆

NOTES AND PHOTOS

INDIANA DUNES NATIONAL PARK, IN

Date visited: .... Weather: ☀ ⛅ ☁ ⛅ 🌧 ⛈ ☁ 🌨 🌨

Traveling companions: ....

Where we stayed: ....

What we did: ....

....

....

....

....

Sights seen: ....

....

....

....

Wildlife seen: ....

....

....

....

Favorite moments: ....

....

....

....

....

....

....

....

....

....

....

PASSPORT STAMP(S)

Favorite attractions:

Visit again?

Things to remember for next time:

Park rating: ☆ ☆ ☆ ☆ ☆

NOTES AND PHOTOS

JEAN LAFITTE
NATIONAL HISTORICAL PARK, LA

Date visited: .... Weather: ☀ 🌦 ☁ ⛅ 🌧 ⛈ ☁ 🌨 🌨

Traveling companions: ....

Where we stayed: ....

What we did: ....

....

....

....

Sights seen: ....

....

....

Wildlife seen: ....

....

....

Favorite moments: ....

....

....

....

....

....

....

....

....

PASSPORT STAMP(S)

Favorite attractions:

Visit again?

Things to remember for next time:

Park rating: ☆ ☆ ☆ ☆ ☆

NOTES AND PHOTOS

JOSHUA TREE NATIONAL PARK, CA

Date visited: _____ Weather: ☀ ⛅ ☁ ⛅ 🌧 ⛈ ☁ 🌨 🌨

Traveling companions: _____

Where we stayed: _____

What we did: _____

_____

_____

_____

Sights seen: _____

_____

_____

Wildlife seen: _____

_____

_____

Favorite moments: _____

_____

_____

_____

_____

_____

_____

_____

_____

PASSPORT STAMP(S)

Favorite attractions:

Visit again?

Things to remember for next time:

Park rating: ☆ ☆ ☆ ☆ ☆

NOTES AND PHOTOS

LINCOLN HOME
NATIONAL HISTORIC SITE, IL

Date visited: .... Weather: ☀ ⛅ ☁ ⛅ ☁ ⛈ ☁ ☁ ☁

Traveling companions: ....

Where we stayed: ....

What we did: ....

....

....

Sights seen: ....

....

....

Wildlife seen: ....

....

....

Favorite moments: ....

....

....

....

....

....

....

....

....

....

....

PASSPORT STAMP(S)

Favorite attractions:

Visit again?

Things to remember for next time:

Park rating: ☆ ☆ ☆ ☆ ☆

NOTES AND PHOTOS

LINCOLN MEMORIAL, DC

Date visited: .... Weather: ☀ ⛅ ☁ ⛅ ☁ ⛈ ☁ ☁ ☁

Traveling companions: ....

Where we stayed: ....

What we did: ....

....

....

Sights seen: ....

....

....

Wildlife seen: ....

....

....

Favorite moments: ....

....

....

....

....

....

....

....

....

PASSPORT STAMP(S)

Favorite attractions:

Visit again?

Things to remember for next time:

Park rating: ☆ ☆ ☆ ☆ ☆

NOTES AND PHOTOS

MAMMOTH CAVE NATIONAL PARK, KY

Date visited: _____ Weather: ☀ ⛅ ☁ ⛅ ☁ ⛈ ☁ ❄ 🌨

Traveling companions: _____

Where we stayed: _____

What we did: _____

_____

_____

_____

Sights seen: _____

_____

_____

_____

Wildlife seen: _____

_____

_____

_____

Favorite moments: _____

_____

_____

_____

_____

_____

_____

_____

_____

_____

_____

PASSPORT STAMP(S)

Favorite attractions:

Visit again?

Things to remember for next time:

Park rating: ☆ ☆ ☆ ☆ ☆

NOTES AND PHOTOS

MARSH-BILLINGS-ROCKEFELLER NATIONAL HISTORICAL PARK, VT

Date visited: .... Weather:

Traveling companions: ....

Where we stayed: ....

What we did: ....

....

....

....

Sights seen: ....

....

....

....

Wildlife seen: ....

....

....

....

Favorite moments: ....

....

....

....

....

....

....

....

....

....

....

PASSPORT STAMP(S)

Favorite attractions: ....

....

....

Visit again? ....

Things to remember for next time: ....

....

....

Park rating: ☆ ☆ ☆ ☆ ☆

NOTES AND PHOTOS

....

....

....

....

....

....

....

MARTIN LUTHER KING, JR. MEMORIAL, DC

Date visited: .... Weather: ☀ 🌦 ☁ 🌤 🌧 ⛈ ☁ 🌨 🌨

Traveling companions: ....

Where we stayed: ....

What we did: ....

....

....

Sights seen: ....

....

....

Wildlife seen: ....

....

....

Favorite moments: ....

....

....

....

....

....

....

....

....

PASSPORT STAMP(S)

Favorite attractions:

Visit again?

Things to remember for next time:

Park rating: ☆ ☆ ☆ ☆ ☆

NOTES AND PHOTOS

MESA VERDE NATIONAL PARK, CO

Date visited: .... Weather: ☀ ⛅ ☁ ⛅ 🌧 ⛈ ☁ 🌨 🌨

Traveling companions: ....

Where we stayed: ....

What we did: ....

....

....

....

Sights seen: ....

....

....

Wildlife seen: ....

....

....

Favorite moments: ....

....

....

....

....

....

....

....

....

....

....

PASSPORT STAMP(S)

Favorite attractions:

Visit again?

Things to remember for next time:

Park rating: ☆ ☆ ☆ ☆ ☆

NOTES AND PHOTOS

NATCHEZ TRACE PARKWAY, AL/MS/TN

Date visited: .... Weather: ☀ ⛅ ☁ ⛅ 🌧 ⛈ ☁ 🌨 🌧

Traveling companions: ....

Where we stayed: ....

What we did: ....

....

....

....

Sights seen: ....

....

....

....

Wildlife seen: ....

....

....

....

Favorite moments: ....

....

....

....

....

....

....

....

....

....

....

PASSPORT STAMP(S)

Favorite attractions:

Visit again?

Things to remember for next time:

Park rating: ☆ ☆ ☆ ☆ ☆

NOTES AND PHOTOS

NEW RIVER GORGE NATIONAL PARK, WV

Date visited: .... Weather: ☀ ⛅ ☁ ⛅ 🌧 ⛈ ☁ 🌨 🌨

Traveling companions: ....

Where we stayed: ....

What we did: ....

....

....

....

Sights seen: ....

....

....

Wildlife seen: ....

....

....

Favorite moments: ....

....

....

....

....

....

....

....

....

....

PASSPORT STAMP(S)

Favorite attractions:

Visit again?

Things to remember for next time:

Park rating: ☆ ☆ ☆ ☆ ☆

NOTES AND PHOTOS

NEZ PERCE
NATIONAL HISTORICAL PARK, ID/MT/OR/WA

Date visited: .... Weather: ☀ ⛆ ☁ ⛅ 🌧 ⛈ ☁ ❄ 🌨

Traveling companions: ....

Where we stayed: ....

What we did: ....

....

....

....

Sights seen: ....

....

....

....

Wildlife seen: ....

....

....

....

Favorite moments: ....

....

....

....

....

....

....

....

....

....

PASSPORT STAMP(S)

Favorite attractions:

Visit again?

Things to remember for next time:

Park rating: ☆ ☆ ☆ ☆ ☆

NOTES AND PHOTOS

OCMULGEE MOUNDS
NATIONAL HISTORICAL PARK, GA

Date visited: .... Weather: ☀ ⛅ ☁ ⛅ 🌧 ⛈ ☁ 🌨 🌨

Traveling companions: ....

Where we stayed: ....

What we did: ....

....

....

....

Sights seen: ....

....

....

....

Wildlife seen: ....

....

....

....

Favorite moments: ....

....

....

....

....

....

....

....

....

....

PASSPORT STAMP(S)

Favorite attractions:

Visit again?

Things to remember for next time:

Park rating: ☆ ☆ ☆ ☆ ☆

NOTES AND PHOTOS

OLYMPIC NATIONAL PARK, WA

Date visited: .... Weather: ☀ ⛅ ☁ ⛅ 🌧 ⛈ ☁ ❄ 🌨

Traveling companions: ....

Where we stayed: ....

What we did: ....

....

....

Sights seen: ....

....

....

Wildlife seen: ....

....

....

Favorite moments: ....

....

....

....

....

....

....

....

....

....

PASSPORT STAMP(S)

Favorite attractions:

Visit again?

Things to remember for next time:

Park rating: ☆ ☆ ☆ ☆ ☆

NOTES AND PHOTOS

OZARK
NATIONAL SCENIC RIVERWAYS, MO

Date visited: .... Weather: ☀ ⛅ ☁ ⛅ 🌧 ⛈ ☁ 🌨 🌨

Traveling companions: ....

Where we stayed: ....

What we did: ....

....

....

....

Sights seen: ....

....

....

....

Wildlife seen: ....

....

....

....

Favorite moments: ....

....

....

....

....

....

....

....

....

PASSPORT STAMP(S)

Favorite attractions:

Visit again?

Things to remember for next time:

Park rating: ☆ ☆ ☆ ☆ ☆

NOTES AND PHOTOS

PICTURED ROCKS
NATIONAL LAKESHORE, MI

Date visited: .... Weather:

Traveling companions: ....

Where we stayed: ....

What we did: ....

....

....

....

Sights seen: ....

....

....

Wildlife seen: ....

....

....

Favorite moments: ....

....

....

....

....

....

....

....

....

....

....

PASSPORT STAMP(S)

Favorite attractions:

Visit again?

Things to remember for next time:

Park rating: ☆ ☆ ☆ ☆ ☆

NOTES AND PHOTOS

REDWOOD NATIONAL AND STATE PARKS, CA

Date visited: .... Weather: ☀ ⛅ ☁ ⛅ ☁ ⛈ ☁ ❄ ❄

Traveling companions: ....

Where we stayed: ....

What we did: ....

....

....

....

Sights seen: ....

....

....

Wildlife seen: ....

....

....

Favorite moments: ....

....

....

....

....

....

....

....

....

....

PASSPORT STAMP(S)

Favorite attractions:

Visit again?

Things to remember for next time:

Park rating: ☆ ☆ ☆ ☆ ☆

NOTES AND PHOTOS

ROCKY MOUNTAIN NATIONAL PARK, CO

Date visited: .... Weather:

Traveling companions: ....

Where we stayed: ....

What we did: ....

....

....

....

Sights seen: ....

....

....

Wildlife seen: ....

....

....

Favorite moments: ....

....

....

....

....

....

....

....

....

....

....

PASSPORT STAMP(S)

Favorite attractions:

Visit again?

Things to remember for next time:

Park rating: ☆ ☆ ☆ ☆ ☆

NOTES AND PHOTOS

ROGER WILLIAMS
NATIONAL MEMORIAL, RI

Date visited: .... Weather: ☀ ⛅ ☁ 🌤 🌧 ⛈ ☁ 🌨 🌨

Traveling companions: ....

Where we stayed: ....

What we did: ....

....

....

....

Sights seen: ....

....

....

....

Wildlife seen: ....

....

....

....

Favorite moments: ....

....

....

....

....

....

....

....

....

....

....

PASSPORT STAMP(S)

Favorite attractions:

Visit again?

Things to remember for next time:

Park rating: ☆ ☆ ☆ ☆ ☆

NOTES AND PHOTOS

SAINT CROIX
NATIONAL SCENIC RIVERWAY, MN/WI

Date visited: .... Weather:

Traveling companions: ....

Where we stayed: ....

What we did: ....

....

....

Sights seen: ....

....

....

Wildlife seen: ....

....

....

Favorite moments: ....

....

....

....

....

....

....

....

....

....

....

PASSPORT STAMP(S)

Favorite attractions:

Visit again?

Things to remember for next time:

Park rating: ☆ ☆ ☆ ☆ ☆

NOTES AND PHOTOS

SAINT-GAUDENS
NATIONAL HISTORICAL PARK, NH

Date visited: .... Weather: ☀ ⛅ ☁ ⛅ 🌧 ⛈ ☁ 🌨 🌨

Traveling companions: ....

Where we stayed: ....

What we did: ....

....

....

....

Sights seen: ....

....

....

....

Wildlife seen: ....

....

....

....

Favorite moments: ....

....

....

....

....

....

....

....

....

....

PASSPORT STAMP(S)

Favorite attractions: ....

....

....

Visit again? ....

Things to remember for next time: ....

....

....

Park rating:

NOTES AND PHOTOS

SAN FRANCISCO MARITIME
NATIONAL HISTORICAL PARK, CA

Date visited: _____ Weather:

Traveling companions: _____

Where we stayed: _____

What we did: _____

_____

_____

Sights seen: _____

_____

_____

Wildlife seen: _____

_____

_____

Favorite moments: _____

_____

_____

_____

_____

_____

_____

_____

_____

_____

PASSPORT STAMP(S)

Favorite attractions:

Visit again?

Things to remember for next time:

Park rating: ☆ ☆ ☆ ☆ ☆

NOTES AND PHOTOS

SCOTTS BLUFF NATIONAL MONUMENT, NE

Date visited: .... Weather: ☀ 🌦 ☁ 🌤 🌧 ⛈ 🌥 🌨 🌨

Traveling companions: ....

Where we stayed: ....

What we did: ....

....

....

Sights seen: ....

....

....

Wildlife seen: ....

....

....

Favorite moments: ....

....

....

....

....

....

....

....

....

....

....

PASSPORT STAMP(S)

Favorite attractions:

Visit again?

Things to remember for next time:

Park rating: ☆ ☆ ☆ ☆ ☆

NOTES AND PHOTOS

SHENANDOAH NATIONAL PARK, VA

Date visited: .... Weather: ☀ ⛈ ☁ ⛅ ☁ ⛈ ☁ ❄ 🌨

Traveling companions: ....

Where we stayed: ....

What we did: ....

....

....

....

Sights seen: ....

....

....

Wildlife seen: ....

....

....

Favorite moments: ....

....

....

....

....

....

....

....

....

....

PASSPORT STAMP(S)

Favorite attractions:

Visit again?

Things to remember for next time:

Park rating: ☆ ☆ ☆ ☆ ☆

NOTES AND PHOTOS

SLEEPING BEAR DUNES
NATIONAL LAKESHORE, MI

Date visited: .... Weather: ☀ ⛅ ☁ ⛅ ☁ ⛈ ☁ ❄ 🌨

Traveling companions: ....

Where we stayed: ....

What we did: ....

....

....

Sights seen: ....

....

....

Wildlife seen: ....

....

....

Favorite moments: ....

....

....

....

....

....

....

....

....

....

PASSPORT STAMP(S)

Favorite attractions:

Visit again?

Things to remember for next time:

Park rating: ☆ ☆ ☆ ☆ ☆

NOTES AND PHOTOS

TALLGRASS PRAIRIE
NATIONAL PRESERVE, KS

Date visited: .... Weather: ☀ ⛅ ☁ ⛅ 🌧 ⛈ ☁ 🌨 🌨

Traveling companions: ....

Where we stayed: ....

What we did: ....

....

....

....

Sights seen: ....

....

....

....

Wildlife seen: ....

....

....

....

Favorite moments: ....

....

....

....

....

....

....

....

....

....

....

PASSPORT STAMP(S)

Favorite attractions:

Visit again?

Things to remember for next time:

Park rating: ☆ ☆ ☆ ☆ ☆

NOTES AND PHOTOS

THEODORE ROOSEVELT
NATIONAL PARK, ND

Date visited: .... Weather: ☀ ⛅ ☁ ⛅ 🌧 ⛈ ☁ 🌨 🌨

Traveling companions: ....

Where we stayed: ....

What we did: ....

....

....

Sights seen: ....

....

....

Wildlife seen: ....

....

....

Favorite moments: ....

....

....

....

....

....

....

....

....

PASSPORT STAMP(S)

Favorite attractions: ....

....

....

Visit again? ....

Things to remember for next time: ....

....

....

Park rating: ☆ ☆ ☆ ☆ ☆

NOTES AND PHOTOS

....

....

....

....

....

....

VOYAGEURS NATIONAL PARK, MN

Date visited: .... Weather: ☀ ⛅ ☁ ⛅ 🌧 ⛈ ☁ 🌨 🌨

Traveling companions: ....

Where we stayed: ....

What we did: ....

....

....

....

Sights seen: ....

....

....

....

Wildlife seen: ....

....

....

....

Favorite moments: ....

....

....

....

....

....

....

....

....

....

....

PASSPORT STAMP(S)

Favorite attractions:

Visit again?

Things to remember for next time:

Park rating: ☆ ☆ ☆ ☆ ☆

NOTES AND PHOTOS

WASHITA BATTLEFIELD
NATIONAL HISTORIC SITE, OK

Date visited: .... Weather: ☀ ⛅ ☁ ⛅ 🌧 ⛈ ☁ 🌨 🌨

Traveling companions: ....

Where we stayed: ....

What we did: ....

....

....

....

Sights seen: ....

....

....

Wildlife seen: ....

....

....

Favorite moments: ....

....

....

....

....

....

....

....

....

PASSPORT STAMP(S)

Favorite attractions:

Visit again?

Things to remember for next time:

Park rating: ☆ ☆ ☆ ☆ ☆

NOTES AND PHOTOS

WEIR FARM NATIONAL HISTORIC SITE, CT

Date visited: _____ Weather: ☀ ⛅ ☁ ⛅ 🌧 ⛈ ☁ 🌨 🌨

Traveling companions: _____

Where we stayed: _____

What we did: _____

_____

_____

Sights seen: _____

_____

_____

Wildlife seen: _____

_____

_____

Favorite moments: _____

_____

_____

_____

_____

_____

_____

_____

_____

_____

PASSPORT STAMP(S)

Favorite attractions:

Visit again?

Things to remember for next time:

Park rating: ☆ ☆ ☆ ☆ ☆

NOTES AND PHOTOS

WHITE SANDS NATIONAL PARK, NM

Date visited: .... Weather:

Traveling companions: ....

Where we stayed: ....

What we did: ....

....

....

Sights seen: ....

....

....

Wildlife seen: ....

....

....

Favorite moments: ....

....

....

....

....

....

....

....

....

....

PASSPORT STAMP(S)

Favorite attractions:

Visit again?

Things to remember for next time:

Park rating: ☆ ☆ ☆ ☆ ☆

NOTES AND PHOTOS

YELLOWSTONE
NATIONAL PARK, ID/MT/WY

Date visited: .... Weather:

Traveling companions: ....

Where we stayed: ....

What we did: ....

....

....

Sights seen: ....

....

....

Wildlife seen: ....

....

....

Favorite moments: ....

....

....

....

....

....

....

....

....

PASSPORT STAMP(S)

Favorite attractions:

Visit again?

Things to remember for next time:

Park rating: ☆ ☆ ☆ ☆ ☆

NOTES AND PHOTOS

YOSEMITE NATIONAL PARK, CA

Date visited: .... Weather:

Traveling companions: ....

Where we stayed: ....

What we did: ....

....

....

Sights seen: ....

....

....

Wildlife seen: ....

....

....

Favorite moments: ....

....

....

....

....

....

....

....

....

....

PASSPORT STAMP(S)

Favorite attractions: ....

....

....

Visit again? ....

Things to remember for next time: ....

....

....

Park rating: ☆ ☆ ☆ ☆ ☆

NOTES AND PHOTOS

....

....

....

....

....

....

ZION NATIONAL PARK, UT

Date visited: .... Weather: ☀ ⛅ ☁ ⛅ 🌧 ⛈ ☁ 🌨 🌧

Traveling companions: ....

Where we stayed: ....

What we did: ....

....

....

....

Sights seen: ....

....

....

Wildlife seen: ....

....

....

Favorite moments: ....

....

....

....

....

....

....

....

....

....

....

PASSPORT STAMP(S)

Favorite attractions:

Visit again?

Things to remember for next time:

Park rating: ☆ ☆ ☆ ☆ ☆

NOTES AND PHOTOS

SAN JUAN NATIONAL HISTORIC SITE, PR

Date visited: _____ Weather: ☀ ⛅ ☁ ⛅ ☁ ⛈ ☁ 🌨 🌨

Traveling companions: _____

Where we stayed: _____

What we did: _____

_____

_____

Sights seen: _____

_____

_____

Wildlife seen: _____

_____

_____

Favorite moments: _____

_____

_____

_____

_____

_____

_____

_____

_____

PASSPORT STAMP(S)

Favorite attractions:

Visit again?

Things to remember for next time:

Park rating: ☆ ☆ ☆ ☆ ☆

NOTES AND PHOTOS